Under My Feet

Moles

Patricia Whitehouse

Heinemann Library
Chicago, Illinois

Customer Service 888-454-2279
Visit our website at www.heinemannlibrary.com

Designed by Sue Emerson, Heinemann Library; Page layout by Que-Net Media™
Printed and bound in the United States by Lake Book Manufacturing, Inc.
Photo research by Bill Broyles

08 07 06 05 04
10 9 8 7 6 5 4 3 2 1

Library of Congress Cataloging-in-Publication Data
Whitehouse, Patricia, 1958-
  Moles / Patricia Whitehouse.
     v. cm. – (Under my feet)
Contents: Do moles live here? – What are moles? – What do moles look like? – Where do moles live? – What do mole homes look like? – How do moles find their way underground? – How do moles make their homes? – What is special about mole homes? – When do moles come out from underground? – Mole home map.
  ISBN 1-4034-4317-3 (HC), 1-4034-4326-2 (Pbk.)
  1. Moles (Animals)–Juvenile literature. [1. Moles (Animals)] I. Title.
  QL737.I57.W47 2003
  599.33'5–dc21

                                   2003000037

Acknowledgments
The author and publishers are grateful to the following for permission to reproduce copyright material:
p. 4 Digital Vision/Getty Images; p. 5 Gregory K. Scott/Photo Researchers, Inc.; p. 6 Marian Bacon/Animals Animals/Earth Scenes; p. 7 Oxford Scientific Films; pp. 8, 15, 18, 19, 21 Dwight Kuhn; p. 9 Photo Researchers, Inc.; p. 10 Steve Maslowski/Photo Researchers, Inc.; p. 11L Corbis; p. 11R C. McIntyre/PhotoLink/Getty Images; p. 12 Jean Philippe/Photo Researchers, Inc.; p. 13 D. Cavagnaro/DRK Photo; p. 14 Leonard Lee Rue III/Visuals Unlimited; p. 16 Jeffrey L. Rotman/Corbis; p. 16 Stephen Dalton/NHPA; pp. 17, 20 Hans Reinhard/Bruce Coleman Inc.; p. 23 (row 1, L-R) Steve Maslowski/Photo Researchers, Inc., Hans Reinhard/Bruce Coleman Inc., Jean Philippe/Photo Researchers, Inc.; (row 2, L-R) Corbis, Photo Researchers, Inc., D. Cavagnaro/DRK Photo; (row 3) Marian Bacon/Animals Animals/Earth Scenes; back cover (L-R) Hans Reinhard/Bruce Coleman Inc., Photo Researchers, Inc.

Illustration on page 22 by Will Hobbs
Cover photograph by Manfred Danegger/OKAPIA/Photo Researchers, Inc.

Special thanks to our advisory panel for their help in the preparation of this book:

Alice Bethke, Library Consultant
Palo Alto, CA

Eileen Day, Preschool Teacher
Chicago, IL

Kathleen Gilbert,
Second Grade Teacher
Round Rock, TX

Sandra Gilbert,
Library Media Specialist
Fiest Elementary School
Houston, TX

Jan Gobeille,
Kindergarten Teacher
Garfield Elementary
Oakland, CA

Angela Leeper,
Educational Consultant
Wake Forest, NC

Special thanks to Mark Rosenthal, Abra Prentice Wilkin Curator of Large Mammals at Chicago's Lincoln Park Zoo, for his help in the preparation of this book.

Some words are shown in bold, **like this.**
You can find them in the picture glossary on page 23.

Contents

Do Moles Live Here?

When you walk outside, you might not see a mole.

But you might be walking over one.

Moles live under your feet.

Their homes are underground.

What Are Moles?

Moles are **mammals.**

Mammals have hair or fur on their bodies.

Mammals make milk for their babies.

These are new baby moles.

What Do Moles Look Like?

claw   eye   paw

Moles have tiny eyes.

They have short legs and big front paws with long claws.

snout

Moles have long **snouts** and pointy teeth.

Most moles are about the size of a kitten.

Where Do Moles Live?

Most moles live alone underground.

Their homes are called **burrows**.

Some moles live in places with trees or rivers.

Some live in **deserts**.

What Do Mole Homes Look Like?

Most mole homes have **tunnels.**

There are special rooms for sleeping.

Some mole homes have
many tunnels.

You can see the **tunnel ridges**
above the ground.

How Do They Find Their Way?

Most moles cannot see well.

This kind of mole cannot see at all.

Moles use their noses to smell.

This mole has special parts on its nose that help it find food.

How Do Moles Make Their Homes?

Moles dig dirt with their front paws.

They push the dirt outside.

The dirt piles up around the hole.

The piles of dirt are called **molehills**.

What Is Special About Their Homes?

Mole **tunnels** are traps for food.

Bugs and worms fall through the dirt into the tunnels.

The mole finds the bugs or worms.

Then, the mole eats them.

When Do Moles Come Out from Underground?

Most moles do not come out of their **burrows.**

They cannot move quickly or see above ground.

Some moles come out to find food.

This mole swims to find food!

Mole Home Map

tunnel ridges

molehill

tunnel

Picture Glossary

burrow
pages 10, 20

molehill
pages 17, 22

tunnel
pages 12, 13,
18, 22

desert
page 11

snout
page 9

**tunnel
ridges**
pages 13, 22

mammal
pages 6, 7

Note to Parents and Teachers

Reading for information is an important part of a child's literacy development. Learning begins with a question about something. Help children think of themselves as investigators and researchers by encouraging their questions about the world around them. Each chapter in this book begins with a question. Read the question together. Look at the pictures. Talk about what you think the answer might be. Then read the text to find out if your predictions were correct. Think of other questions you could ask about the topic, and discuss where you might find the answers. Assist children in using the picture glossary and the index to practice new vocabulary and research skills.

❗ CAUTION: Remind children that it is not a good idea to handle wild animals or insects. Children should wash their hands with soap and water after they touch any animal.

Index